Get **A**rt Sma

What Is Color?

by Tea Benduhn

Crabtree Publishing Company
www.crabtreebooks.com

Crabtree Publishing Company

Author: Tea Benduhn
Publishing plan research and development:
  Sean Charlebois, Reagan Miller
  Crabtree Publishing Company
Editors: Reagan Miller
Proofreader: Kathy Middleton, Molly Aloian
Editorial director: Kathy Middleton
Photo research: Edward A. Thomas
Designer: Tammy West, Westgraphix LLC
Production coordinator: Margaret Amy Salter
Prepress technician: Margaret Amy Salter
Consultant: Julie Collins-Dutkiewicz, B.A., specialist in early
  childhood education, Sandy Waite, M.Ed., U.S. National
  Board Certified Teacher, author, and literacy consultant
Reading Consultant: Susan Nations, M.Ed., Author/
  Literacy Coach/Consultant in Literacy Development

Photographs and reproductions
Cover: iStock; 1: Shuttersotock; 5: © Marcelo Rudini/Alamy; 7,
9: iStockphoto; 13: Image Club Graphics: Circa Art; 15: Art
Institute of Chicago/The Bridgeman Art Library; 17: Private
Collection/Peter Willi/The Bridgeman Art Library; 19: The
Israel Museum, Jerusalem/Gift of Yad Hanadiv, Jerusalem,
from the collection of Miriam Alexandrine de Rothschild/The
Bridgeman Art Library; 21: Private Collection/The Bridgeman
Art Library; 23: Metropolitan Museum of Art, New York/
Lauros/Giraudon/The Bridgeman Art Library.

Front cover (main image): A young artist proudly displays her work.
Title page: Two young artists experiment with paints.

Written, developed, and produced by RJF Publishing LLC

Library and Archives Canada Cataloguing in Publication

Benduhn, Tea
    What is color? / Tea Benduhn.

(Get art smart)
Includes index.
ISBN 978-0-7787-5123-6 (bound).--ISBN 978-0-7787-5137-3 (pbk.)

    1. Color in art--Juvenile literature. I. Title. II. Series: Get art smart

N7432.7.B45 2009   j701'.85   C2009-903591-X

Library of Congress Cataloging-in-Publication Data

Benduhn, Tea.

    What is color? / Tea Benduhn.
        p. cm. -- (Get art smart)
    Includes index.
    ISBN 978-0-7787-5137-3 (pbk. : alk. paper) -- ISBN 978-0-7787-5123-6
(reinforced library binding : alk. paper)
    1. Color in art--Juvenile literature. I. Title. II. Series.

N7432.7.B46 2009
701'.85--dc22
                                              2009022914

Crabtree Publishing Company
www.crabtreebooks.com   1-800-387-7650

Printed in the U.S.A./052014/CJ20140421

**Published
in Canada
Crabtree Publishing**
616 Welland Ave.
St. Catharines, Ontario
L2M 5V6

**Published in
the United States
Crabtree Publishing**
PMB 59051
350 Fifth Avenue, 59th Floor
New York, New York 10118

**Published in the
United Kingdom
Crabtree Publishing**
Maritime House
Basin Road North, Hove
BN41 1WR

**Published
in Australia
Crabtree Publishing**
3 Charles Street
Coburg North
VIC, 3058

Contents

Color Everywhere 4

Primary Colors 6

Secondary Colors. 8

The Color Wheel 10

Complementary Colors. 12

Colors in Art. 14

Black and White 16

Warm Colors 18

Cool Colors 20

Name the Colors 22

Words to Know and Find Out More 24

Color Everywhere

When the lights are off at night, everything looks gray or black. You can see color when there is light. You can see color at home, at school, and outside. Everywhere you look, objects have color.

The walls in this classroom are yellow.
What color are the walls in your classroom?

Some colors are called **primary colors**. Blue, red, and yellow are the three primary colors. Every other color you see is made of these colors.

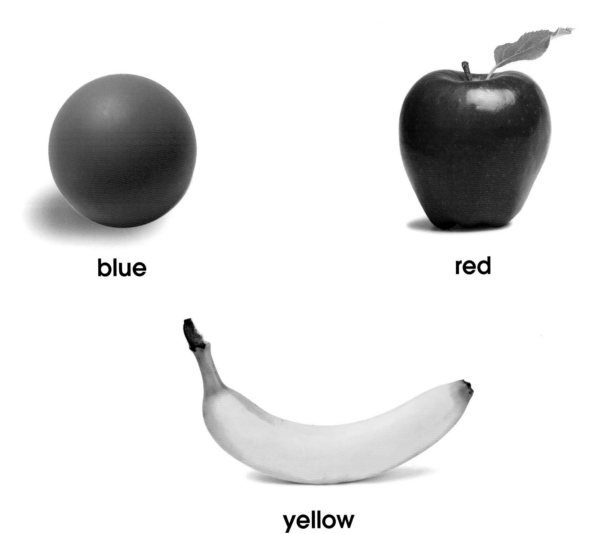

blue

red

yellow

Look around you. Do you see objects that are blue, red, or yellow?

Some colors are called **secondary colors**. Orange, green, and purple are the three secondary colors. Purple is also called violet. Two primary colors are mixed together to make a secondary color.

These crayons were made in the three secondary colors.

The Color Wheel

A **color wheel** shows primary colors and secondary colors. Secondary colors are between the primary colors that are used to make them. Orange is between red and yellow on the color wheel. Red and yellow are mixed together to make orange.

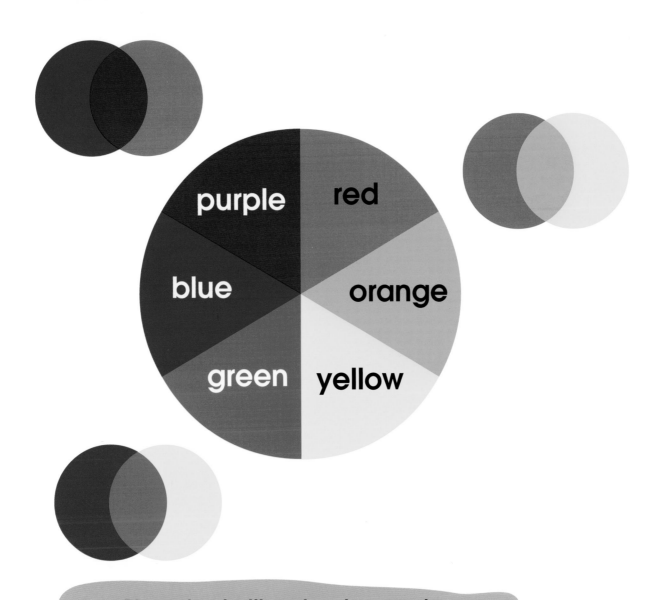

Blue mixed with red makes purple.
Red mixed with yellow makes orange.
Blue mixed with yellow makes green.

11

Complementary Colors

Complementary colors are opposite each other on the color wheel. Blue and orange are opposite each other. They are complementary colors. When you put two complementary colors next to each other, each color makes the other one look brighter.

Crown Imperial Fritillaries in a Copper Vase, by Vincent van Gogh (1886)

The artist used the complementary colors blue and orange for the wall and the flowers in this painting.

13

Colors in Art

We can use color when we make art. We can use colored pencils, chalk, markers, and crayons to draw pictures. We can use colors of paint to make paintings. We can use colors to show feelings. We can use bright colors to show that people in a picture are happy.

Two Sisters, or On the Terrace, by Pierre Auguste Renoir (1881)

Look at the colors in this picture. How do you think the people in the picture feel?

Black and White

We can add black or white to change colors. We can mix black with colors to make **shades**. If you add black to red, you make the color **burgundy**. Burgundy is a shade of red. We can mix white with colors to make **tints**. We can mix white with red to make pink. Pink is a tint of red.

The Dance of the Moulin Rouge (detail),
by Henri de Toulouse-Lautrec (1889)

The artist mixed white with red to make the pink color of this woman's coat.

Warm Colors

The colors red, yellow, and orange are called **warm colors**. Warm colors are like the sun. They create a feeling of warmth. We can use warm colors to make people who look at a painting feel warm.

Harvest in Provence, by Vincent van Gogh (1888)

Look at the painting. Do the colors make you think that it is a hot day?

Cool Colors

Colors that have blue in them are called **cool colors**. Green, blue, and violet are cool colors. Cool colors are like water. They create a cool feeling.

Water Lilies, by Claude Monet (late 1800s or early 1900s)

Does the blue water in this painting make you feel cool?

21

Name the Colors

Now you know how to use color to make art. How many colors do you see in this painting? Are they primary colors or secondary colors? Do you see warm colors? Do you see cool colors? Do you see shades or tints?

The Terrace at Sainte-Adresse, by Claude Monet (1867)

The artist used many different colors in this painting.

Words to Know

cool colors

blue   red   yellow

primary colors

orange green purple

secondary colors

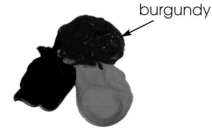

burgundy

shade

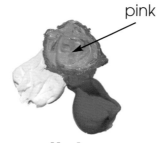

pink

tint

warm colors

Find Out More

Books

Micklethwait, Lucy. *I Spy Colors in Art*. New York: Greenwillow Books, 2007.

Yenawine, Philip. *Colors*. New York: Museum of Modern Art, 2006.

Web sites

A Lifetime of Color
www.alifetimeofcolor.com

Enchanted Learning—color activities
www.enchantedlearning.com/themes/colors.shtml